BRING
IN THE
GLORY

BRING IN THE GLORY

Worshipping in the Heavenly Temple

H.L. ROBERTSON

Bring in the Glory
Copyright © 2016 by H.L. Robertson. All rights reserved.

No part of this publication may be reproduced, stored in a retrieval system or transmitted in any way by any means, electronic, mechanical, photocopy, recording or otherwise without the prior permission of the author except as provided by USA copyright law.

Scripture quotations marked (KJV) are taken from the *Holy Bible, King James Version*, Cambridge, 1769. Used by permission. All rights reserved.

Fairhaven Media, Lynchburg, TN

Cover design by Joshua Rafols
Interior design by Shieldon Alcasid

Published in the United States of America
ISBN: 978-0-9987480-8-5

1. Religion / Biblical Criticism & Interpretation / General
2. Religion / Biblical Commentary / General
16.03.31

To all those hungry souls who, like me,
have found freedom and joy in Abba's throne room

Contents

Introduction 11

1 Heavenly Jerusalem 19
2 The Heavenly Temple 29
3 The Lord Enthroned in Heaven 41
4 Entering Heavenly Places 47
5 The Heavenly Angels 53
6 Kings and Priests 63
7 Participating in the Heavenly Worship 71
8 At the Right Hand 79
9 The Veil Is Torn 85
10 Davidic Worship 91
11 Bringing in the Glory 99

Then went up Moses, and Aaron, Nadab, and Abihu, and seventy of the elders of Israel: And they saw the God of Israel: and there was under his feet as it were a paved work of a sapphire stone, and as it were the body of heaven in his clearness. And upon the nobles of the children of Israel he laid not his hand: also they saw God, and did eat and drink.

Introduction

THERE HAVE BEEN many books written on "the glory." It isn't enough, however, to merely talk about the glory of God. We must acquaint ourselves with the implications of bringing in the glory and what transpires in the heavenlies when we do. We need to understand not only how earth touches heaven but how the heavenly realm reciprocates and manifests itself in the earth.

As we begin to look at the idea of bringing in the glory of God's presence, we first need to understand exactly what God's plan for mankind was and is. This is crucially important, because as fallen human beings, looking at the subject from a viewpoint thousands of years removed from the initial events, we tend to get self-focused and see things through the lens of our circumstances and spiritual realities. God's plan is, and always has been, to have a deep intimate fellowship and relationship with his creation. I have heard it said and taught many, many times: "If you want to know God's plan for mankind, look at the first two chapters of Genesis and the last two chapters of Revelation." Genesis chapters 1 and 2 give us the initial picture of man's creation and God placing him in paradise:

> And God said, Let us make man in our image, after our likeness… (Gen. 1:26)
>
> And the Lord God formed man of the dust of the ground, and breathed into his nostrils the breath of life; and man became a living soul. And the Lord God planted a garden eastward in Eden; and there he put the man whom he had formed. (Gen. 2:7–8)

In the book of Revelation's final chapters, man is once again restored to paradise:

> And I saw a new heaven and a new earth: for the first heaven and the first earth were passed away; and there was no more sea. And I John saw the holy city, new Jerusalem, coming down from God out of heaven, prepared as a bride adorned for her husband. And I heard a great voice out of heaven saying, Behold, the tabernacle of God is with men, and he will dwell with them, and they shall be his people, and God himself shall be with them, and be their God. And God shall wipe away all tears from their eyes; and there shall be no more death, neither sorrow, nor crying, neither shall there be any more pain: for the former things are passed away. And he that sat upon the throne said, Behold, I make all things new. (Rev. 21:1–5)
>
> And he shewed me a pure river of water of life, clear as crystal, proceeding out of the throne of God and of the Lamb. In the midst of the street of it, and on either side of the river, was there the tree of life,

> which bare twelve manner of fruits, and yielded her fruit every month: and the leaves of the tree were for the healing of the nations. And there shall be no more curse: but the throne of God and of the Lamb shall be in it; and his servants shall serve him: And they shall see his face; and his name shall be in their foreheads. And there shall be no night there; and they need no candle, neither light of the sun; for the Lord God giveth them light: and they shall reign for ever and ever. (Rev. 22:1–5)

Man was created in the image of God for a specific purpose: to fellowship with him and have a relationship with him. Genesis 3 shows us a scene in which God, even though he knows man has sinned, came "walking in the garden." The Lord was seeking out his creation to begin restoring the fractured fellowship. Incidentally, God was not shocked, surprised, or disheartened when man fell… He knew man would fall! Revelation 13:8 calls Christ the "lamb slain from the foundation of the world." The cross was absolutely not plan "B"; it was the only plan. That plan was for us to be living in a perfect environment and in perfect harmony with our Creator. To this end, all throughout history, God has been bridging the gap between mankind and himself at every opportunity.

In Genesis 5:24, we are told,

> And Enoch walked with God: and he was not; for God took him.

This short narrative takes place only six generations after Adam. It is as if God was so delighted to have a man who would walk with him in covenant fellowship that he simply took Enoch on to heaven to be with him. We see a similar idea in Revelation's letters to the seven churches:

> Him that overcometh will I make a pillar in the temple of my God, and he shall go no more out… Behold, I stand at the door, and knock: if any man hear my voice, and open the door, I will come in to him, and will sup with him, and he with me. To him that overcometh will I grant to sit with me in my throne, even as I also overcame, and am set down with my Father in his throne. (Rev. 3:12, 20–21)

The first part of these verses gives us a picture of the Lord refusing to even let these overcoming saints leave his presence. They are constantly in his glorious presence in the heavenly temple. The second part shows us God desiring to have a meal with his children. In the Middle Eastern cultures of that day, inviting someone to a meal in your home was one of the most intensely intimate gestures you could make. Having a meal was not just eating and drinking; it was a fellowship encounter. In what is probably the first instance in scripture of a "theophany," a preincarnate appearance of Christ to men, he fellowshipped over a meal with Abraham while discussing the fate of Sodom and Gomorrah:

> And the Lord appeared unto him in the plains of Mamre: and he sat in the tent door in the heat of the day...And said, My Lord, if now I have found favour in thy sight, pass not away, I pray thee, from thy servant: Let a little water, I pray you, be fetched, and wash your feet, and rest yourselves under the tree: And I will fetch a morsel of bread, and comfort ye your hearts...And the Lord said, Because the cry of Sodom and Gomorrah is great, and because their sin is very grievous; I will go down now, and see whether they have done altogether according to the cry of it, which is come unto me; and if not, I will know. (Gen. 18:1, 3–5, 20–21)

This was also the very first manner in which God revealed himself to the leaders of Israel after the exodus from Egypt. At Mount Sinai, while in the process of establishing the Mosaic covenant, we find this narrative:

> Then went up Moses, and Aaron, Nadab, and Abihu, and seventy of the elders of Israel: And they saw the God of Israel: and there was under his feet as it were a paved work of a sapphire stone, and as it were the body of heaven in his clearness. And upon the nobles of the children of Israel he laid not his hand: also they saw God, and did eat and drink. (Exod. 24:9–11)

This, even though the Israelites had just rejected God's personal presence in chapter 20:

> And all the people saw the thunderings, and the lightnings, and the noise of the trumpet, and the mountain smoking: and when the people saw it, they removed, and stood afar off. And they said unto Moses, Speak thou with us, and we will hear: but let not God speak with us, lest we die. (Exod. 20:19)

Just as this pattern of God actively seeking relationship and fellowship with mankind was established almost immediately after the fall, so too this pattern of mankind working to avoid these very types of encounters is seen just as frequently. In Genesis 3:8 (previously referenced), Adam and Eve withdrew from their normal daily fellowship with God; they hid themselves "from the presence of the Lord God." The Hebrew word for *presence* is *paniym*. This word literally means *face*. They hid themselves from the face of God. Exodus 33:20 tells us that no man can (now) look at God's face and live. That is the root of the fall—separation from and loss of a relationship and fellowship with God. In the end, that is exactly what hell consists of—a final and eternal separation from our Creator!

We as fallen humans have lost our ability to physically come into his presence, but through prayer and worship, we who are believers in Jesus Christ can do so spiritually.

That is the heart of what this book is about: the act of entering in. We need to bring in of the glory so as to step into the heavenlies spiritually and come before his face in restored fellowship.

1

Heavenly Jerusalem

IN THE INTRODUCTION, I quoted the following scripture as part of an illustration of God's desire to have fellowship with his creation. Look again at this passage, and notice the mention of "New Jerusalem":

> Him that overcometh will I make a pillar in the temple of my God, and he shall go no more out: and I will write upon him the name of my God, and the name of the city of my God, which is New Jerusalem, which cometh down out of heaven from my God: and I will write upon him my new name. (Rev. 3:12)

We are told repeatedly in scripture that the earthly forms and manners of worship are simply shadows and symbols of the true worship that are carried out in the heavenly realm. This holds true not only of the worship patterns but of all things spiritual. In each case, we will find that the earthly things are a faint copy of those found in the heavenly realm.

Now we will examine the progression of this idea to its climactic fulfillment. First we see the earthly:

> And Ahijah caught the new garment that was on him, and rent it in twelve pieces: And he said to Jeroboam, Take thee ten pieces: for thus saith the LORD, the God of Israel, Behold, I will rend the kingdom out of the hand of Solomon, and will give ten tribes to thee: (But he shall have one tribe for my servant David's sake, and for Jerusalem's sake, the city which I have chosen out of all the tribes of Israel:) Howbeit I will not take the whole kingdom out of his hand: but I will make him prince all the days of his life for David my servant's sake, whom I chose, because he kept my commandments and my statutes: But I will take the kingdom out of his son's hand, and will give it unto thee, even ten tribes. And unto his son will I give one tribe, that David my servant may have a light always before me in Jerusalem, the city which I have chosen me to put my name there. (1 Kings 11:34–36)

And again

> And Rehoboam the son of Solomon reigned in Judah. Rehoboam was forty and one years old when he began to reign, and he reigned seventeen years in Jerusalem, the city which the Lord did choose out of all the tribes of Israel, to put his name there. (1 Kings 14:21)

In these passages, we find God specifically calling the earthly Jerusalem the place where he has chosen to put his name. In other words, this was his earthly headquarters and the site from which his interaction with mankind would be carried out. Both scriptural and historical evidence shows us that Jerusalem was originally a Jebusite city that persisted unconquered in the Promised Land (Josh. 15:63) and was eventually taken by Israel in the time of the Judges (Judg. 1:8, 21). The stronghold of Zion, later the city of David, was not taken until centuries later by David's men (2 Sam. 5:6–10). God, in his foreknowledge, orchestrated the capture and development of the city and later its temple as a reflection of the "Heavenly Jerusalem." It eventually contained both the temple; again a shadow of the heavenly temple (more on this in chapter 2); and the throne of King David, God's regent on the earth. Notice that we have no record that King Saul, the king of Israel's rebellion, ever ruled in Jerusalem. David began his reign in Hebron and later moved to Jerusalem. This city, however, was a fallen Jerusalem, inhabited by a fallen, sinful people. In the end, this earthly city was allowed to be destroyed, not once but twice, because of the nation of Israel's sin and rebellion.

Hebrews 12 gives us a contrast between the encounter of Moses and the Israelites with God at Mount Sinai, and the heavenly mountain called Sion and the heavenly city:

> For ye are not come unto the mount that might be touched, and that burned with fire, nor unto

> blackness, and darkness, and tempest, And the sound of a trumpet, and the voice of words; which voice they that heard intreated that the word should not be spoken to them any more: (For they could not endure that which was commanded, And if so much as a beast touch the mountain, it shall be stoned, or thrust through with a dart: And so terrible was the sight, that Moses said, I exceedingly fear and quake:) But ye are come unto mount Sion, and unto the city of the living God, the heavenly Jerusalem, and to an innumerable company of angels. (Heb. 12:19–22)

This heavenly Jerusalem is the eternal city of God in the heavenly realm. It was never intended as a dwelling for man but was created as the dwelling of God Almighty and the angelic hosts. As we have previously examined, it was to be the pattern by which all things in the earthly city were produced.

Now we will look at the "New Jerusalem." In Hebrews, we are told that Abraham looked forward to this heavenly city:

> By faith Abraham, when he was called to go out into a place which he should after receive for an inheritance, obeyed; and he went out, not knowing whither he went. By faith he sojourned in the land of promise, as in a strange country, dwelling in tabernacles with Isaac and Jacob, the heirs with him of the same promise: For he looked for a city which

hath foundations, whose builder and maker is God. Through faith also Sara herself received strength to conceive seed, and was delivered of a child when she was past age, because she judged him faithful who had promised. Therefore sprang there even of one, and him as good as dead, so many as the stars of the sky in multitude, and as the sand which is by the sea shore innumerable. These all died in faith, not having received the promises, but having seen them afar off, and were persuaded of them, and embraced them, and confessed that they were strangers and pilgrims on the earth. For they that say such things declare plainly that they seek a country. And truly, if they had been mindful of that country from whence they came out, they might have had opportunity to have returned. But now they desire a better country, that is, an heavenly: wherefore God is not ashamed to be called their God: for he hath prepared for them a city. (Heb. 11:9–16)

Notice that Abraham looked for a heavenly city that he fully understood was being prepared for God's people by the Lord himself. He was an alien and stranger in the land that God had promised him, and understood prophetically that Canaan was only a "down payment" of his final inheritance. In fact, it was centuries before his descendants came into possession of Canaan and eventually Jerusalem as already shown above.

In Hebrews 13, the writer proceeds to contrast the whole sacrificial worship system of the Mosaic law and Aaronic priesthood with that of Christ—culminating in the assertion that we too, as New Testament believers, are looking forward to the new Jerusalem and the heavenly worship that will be performed there.

> We have an altar, whereof they have no right to eat which serve the tabernacle. For the bodies of those beasts, whose blood is brought into the sanctuary by the high priest for sin, are burned without the camp. Wherefore Jesus also, that he might sanctify the people with his own blood, suffered without the gate. Let us go forth therefore unto him without the camp, bearing his reproach. For here have we no continuing city, but we seek one to come. By him therefore let us offer the sacrifice of praise to God continually, that is, the fruit of our lips giving thanks to his name. (Heb. 13:10–15)

The earthly Jerusalem that we now know and the heavenly Jerusalem that now exists will be done away with at the "end of time."

> But the day of the Lord will come as a thief in the night; in the which the heavens shall pass away with a great noise, and the elements shall melt with fervent heat, the earth also and the works that are therein shall be burned up. (2 Pet. 3:10)

This demolition of the existing will be carried out to make way for those things that are to come:

> And I saw a new heaven and a new earth: for the first heaven and the first earth were passed away; and there was no more sea. And I John saw the holy city, new Jerusalem, coming down from God out of heaven, prepared as a bride adorned for her husband. And I heard a great voice out of heaven saying, Behold, the tabernacle of God is with men, and he will dwell with them, and they shall be his people, and God himself shall be with them, and be their God. (Rev. 21:2–3)

Notice that both the earthly city of Jerusalem and the currently existing heavenly city will ultimately be replaced by the New Jerusalem. The sin-corrupted earth and the existing heaven, which has been tainted by sin via Satan's rebellion, will be done away with; and the new city will descend from the new heaven to fulfill both roles. God, in the person of Jesus Christ, will dwell with his redeemed creation in the new city on the new earth. He will rule as the Father's agent in the earth, just as Adam was intended to do, and man will be restored to the fellowship with God he lost in the fall.

Time line of the Earthly, Heavenly, and New Jerusalems

From before creation	Heavenly Jerusalem is the site of God's throne
Prehistory	Jebusite city of Jebus (Jerusalem)
Genesis 12:1–6	Abram/Abraham enters Canaan
Genesis 47	Israel comes into Egypt
Exodus 13:17–22	Israel leaves Egypt in the Exodus
Joshua 15:63	Israel leaves Jerusalem unconquered
Judges 1:8, 21	Main city of Jerusalem is taken, but Zion is unconquered still
2 Samuel 5:6–10	Zion is taken by David's men and becomes his fortress
2 Kings 25:8–10	Jerusalem is destroyed and burned by Nebuchadnezzar
Nehemiah 3	Nehemiah begins to rebuild Jerusalem
Matthew 24	Jesus foretells the destruction of the city (by Romans in 70 AD)

Circa 134 AD	City is rebuilt as Aelia Capitolina, a Roman colony
Middle Ages	City is fought over and rebuilt repeatedly by Turks and Crusaders
June 1967	City is captured by Israel during the "Six-Day War"
1967–present	Modern city is built
Revelation 19	Christ returns bodily to the earth
Revelation 20	Christ enters Jerusalem and sets up his a thousand-year kingdom on earth
Revelation 21:1	Existing heaven and earth are destroyed
Revelation 21:2	New Jerusalem descends to the new earth
Revelation 21:3	Christ establishes his eternal kingdom in New Jerusalem

2

The Heavenly Temple

And Moses came and called for the elders of the people, and laid before their faces all these words which the Lord commanded him. And all the people answered together, and said, All that the Lord hath spoken we will do. And Moses returned the words of the people unto the Lord. And the Lord said unto Moses, Lo, I come unto thee in a thick cloud, that the people may hear when I speak with thee, and believe thee for ever. And Moses told the words of the people unto the Lord. And the Lord said unto Moses, Go unto the people, and sanctify them to day and to morrow, and let them wash their clothes, And be ready against the third day: for the third day the Lord will come down in the sight of all the people upon mount Sinai. And thou shalt set bounds unto the people round about, saying, Take heed to yourselves, that ye go not up into the mount, or touch the border of it: whosoever toucheth the mount shall be surely put to death: There shall not an hand touch it, but he shall surely be stoned, or shot through; whether it be beast or man, it shall not live: when the trumpet soundeth long, they shall come up to the mount. And Moses went down from the mount unto the people, and sanctified the people; and they washed their clothes. And he said unto the people, Be ready against the third day: come not at your wives. And it came to pass on the third day in the morning, that there were thunders and lightnings, and a thick cloud upon the mount, and the voice of the trumpet exceeding loud; so that all the people that was in the camp trembled. And Moses brought forth the people out of the camp to meet with God; and they stood at the nether part of the mount. And mount Sinai was altogether on a smoke, because the LORD descended upon it in fire: and the smoke thereof ascended as the smoke of a furnace, and the whole mount quaked greatly. And when the voice of the trumpet sounded long, and waxed louder and louder, Moses spake, and God answered him by a voice. And the Lord came down upon mount Sinai, on the top of the mount: and the Lord called Moses up to the top of the mount; and Moses went up. (Exod. 19:8–20)

THIS PASSAGE DRAWN from Exodus 19 demonstrates for us perfectly that what Moses and the others experienced at Mount Sinai was, with the exception of the events of Exodus 24, merely a figure of the true things in the heavenlies.

Exodus 24:9–11 records a singular experience that shows us how the lines between heaven and earth can be blurred for a brief season so that God can reveal himself and his glory to mankind. (This episode will be dealt with later in this chapter.) In the Garden of Eden, man fellowshipped with God face-to-face. However, since the fall, man was banished from God's presence and, until Jesus came, had encounters with him only through preincarnate human appearances. Now we see Moses having a relationship with God that is reminiscent of Adam and Eve's. Deuteronomy 34:10 tells us,

> And there arose not a prophet since in Israel like unto Moses, whom the Lord knew face to face…

This is obviously something out of the normal. Moses, who is a figure foreshadowing Christ, is the embodiment of prophet, priest, and king. We see Moses ascending the mountain and ministering before God as the heavenly touches the earthly. This too is a figure of Christ who is ministering in the heavenly temple. God then began to give him the Ten Commandments:

> And God spake all these words, saying, I am the Lord thy God, which have brought thee out of the land of Egypt, out of the house of bondage. Thou shalt have no other gods before me. Thou shalt not make unto thee any graven image, or any likeness of

any thing that is in heaven above, or that is in the earth beneath, or that is in the water under the earth: Thou shalt not bow down thyself to them, nor serve them: for I the Lord thy God am a jealous God, visiting the iniquity of the fathers upon the children unto the third and fourth generation of them that hate me; And shewing mercy unto thousands of them that love me, and keep my commandments. Thou shalt not take the name of the Lord thy God in vain; for the Lord will not hold him guiltless that taketh his name in vain. Remember the sabbath day, to keep it holy. Six days shalt thou labour, and do all thy work: But the seventh day is the sabbath of the Lord thy God: in it thou shalt not do any work, thou, nor thy son, nor thy daughter, thy manservant, nor thy maidservant, nor thy cattle, nor thy stranger that is within thy gates: For in six days the Lord made heaven and earth, the sea, and all that in them is, and rested the seventh day: wherefore the Lord blessed the sabbath day, and hallowed it. Honour thy father and thy mother: that thy days may be long upon the land which the Lord thy God giveth thee. Thou shalt not kill. Thou shalt not commit adultery. Thou shalt not steal. Thou shalt not bear false witness against thy neighbour. Thou shalt not covet thy neighbour's house, thou shalt not covet thy neighbour's wife, nor his manservant, nor his maidservant, nor his ox, nor his ass, nor any thing that is thy neighbour's. (Exod. 20:1–17)

Here Moses is given direct, divine instruction to give the Ten Commandments to Israel. We see a parallel in Jesus's ministry:

> Verily, verily, I say unto you, The Son can do nothing of himself, but what he seeth the Father do… (John 5:19)

Why are these passages so significant? Because up until this point, as previously stated, Moses had been functioning as prophet, priest, and king; just as Jesus, until he came to earth, had been fulfilling all three roles. Thus Jesus's statement in John 5:19 above. This is new territory for him. His modus operandi has drastically changed. In the same way, Moses's MO has just changed in Exodus 20:1–17. Mankind, which has been shut off from direct worship of and fellowship with their Creator since the Fall, now is seeing a partial restoration of that fellowship in the person of Moses. Notice that the Lord gave Moses just the Ten Commandments at this point. These were the basic, most fundamental tenets for being in relationship with a holy God. Notice, however, what transpired next:

> And all the people saw the thunderings, and the lightnings, and the noise of the trumpet, and the mountain smoking: and when the people saw it, they removed, and stood afar off. And they said unto Moses, Speak thou with us, and we will hear: but let not God speak with us, lest we die. And Moses said

unto the people, Fear not: for God is come to prove
you, and that his fear may be before your faces, that
ye sin not. And the people stood afar off, and Moses
drew near unto the thick darkness where God was.
(Exod. 20:18–21)

Here we see Israel's rejection of their God. Just as Adam and Eve believed the serpent's lies that God was not trustworthy and was in reality withholding the fruit of the tree of knowledge; Israel refused to trust God and instead feared him. This caused them to withdraw from the relationship that was offered and to opt instead for a secondhand worship through Moses and eventually through an Aaronic priesthood. Just as in the fall, mankind had once again by his own sinful actions rejected God's person and presence. Notice how the ensuing verses describe it:

And the Lord said unto Moses, Thus thou shalt say
unto the children of Israel, Ye have seen that I have
talked with you from heaven. … Now these are the
judgments which thou shalt set before them. (Exod.
20:22, 21:1)

The law is called "God's judgments" on Israel. From this point on, not only is the relationship with God secondhand, but notice that the role of Moses changes. Moses had been prophet, priest, and king; now we see a distribution of those roles. Moses remains the prophet, but the elders take on a large part of the rulership role, and Aaron and his sons become the priests. The ministry of leading the people to God that was focused in the person of Moses on earth has now become diffused and at arm's length, instead of up close and personal. All this judgment was levied for their rejection of relationship with God.

Now in chapters 21 through 23, God institutes the "Mosaic law." This will eventually grow into the other books of the Torah. Through rabbinical tradition and interpretation, it will grow into many hundreds of laws and statutes for the nation of Israel to follow. Gone was the opportunity for man to have a person-to-person relationship with the Almighty, or was it?

The Lord proceeds to give an invitation to a select group to have an intimate encounter with himself.

Chapter 24 outlines this invitation:

> And he said unto Moses, Come up unto the Lord, thou, and Aaron, Nadab, and Abihu, and seventy of the elders of Israel; and worship ye afar off. And Moses alone shall come near the Lord: but they shall not come nigh; neither shall the people go up with him. And Moses came and told the people all the words of the Lord, and all the judgments: and all the people answered with one voice, and said, All the words which the Lord hath said will we do…Then went up Moses, and Aaron, Nadab, and Abihu, and seventy of the elders of Israel: And they saw the God

> of Israel: and there was under his feet as it were a paved work of a sapphire stone, and as it were the body of heaven in his clearness. And upon the nobles of the children of Israel he laid not his hand: also they saw God, and did eat and drink. (Exod. 24:1–3, 9–11)

After this singular encounter, we see the finality of the gulf between man and God. They can only worship from afar now and not "come near." In the intervening verses 4 through 8, we see Moses's last-recorded sacrifice. The priestly role was completely stripped away from him and given from this point on only to Aaron and his offspring beginning a hierarchical priesthood that would utterly fail to minister to the people and would ultimately enslave them (see Matthew 23:1–33).

> And Moses wrote all the words of the Lord, and rose up early in the morning, and builded an altar under the hill, and twelve pillars, according to the twelve tribes of Israel. And he sent young men of the children of Israel, which offered burnt offerings, and sacrificed peace offerings of oxen unto the Lord. And Moses took half of the blood, and put it in basons; and half of the blood he sprinkled on the altar. And he took the book of the covenant, and read in the audience of the people: and they said, All that the Lord hath said will we do, and be obedient. And Moses took the blood, and sprinkled it on the people, and said, Behold the blood of the covenant, which the Lord hath made with you concerning all these words. (Exod. 24:4–8)

This was Moses's last priestly act before he ascended into the mountain and crossed (briefly) into the heavenly realm. This was a foreshadowing of Jesus's last priestly act:

> Jesus saith unto her, Woman, why weepest thou? whom seekest thou?…Jesus saith unto her, Touch me not; for I am not yet ascended to my Father: but go to my brethren, and say unto them, I ascend unto my Father, and your Father; and to my God, and your God. (John 20:15–17)

Jesus ascended into heaven and presented the sacrifice of his own body and blood in the heavenly temple. This is why he refused to be touched: so as not to be ceremonially defiled. By contrast, later that same day, he openly invited his disciples to touch his wounds and handle him once his priestly duty was fulfilled.

In the same way, the great transition in Moses's ministry and Israel's relationship with God now began. In chapters 25 through 31, God gives Moses the design plans for the Tabernacle and all its furnishings. Hebrews 8 describes it from this perspective:

> Now of the things which we have spoken this is the sum: We have such an high priest, who is set on the right hand of the throne of the Majesty in the heavens; A minister of the sanctuary, and of the true tabernacle, which the Lord pitched, and not man. For every high priest is ordained to offer gifts

and sacrifices: wherefore it is of necessity that this man have somewhat also to offer. For if he were on earth, he should not be a priest, seeing that there are priests that offer gifts according to the law: Who serve unto the example and shadow of heavenly things, as Moses was admonished of God when he was about to make the tabernacle: for, See, saith he, that thou make all things according to the pattern shewed to thee in the mount. (Heb. 8:1–5)

God, knowing that Israel had rejected the direct route to himself, needed a witness on earth of the heavenly temple to enable Aaron and his sons to carry out blood sacrifices to roll forward the nation's sins to the day when they could be fully and finally atoned for. This overarching need is demonstrated in Exodus 32. After Moses's sacrifice in chapter 24, the very next sacrifice recorded is to the "golden calf." The enormity of this rebellion is difficult to overstate. It also demonstrates the need for a constant stream of offerings and sacrifices to atone (temporarily) for the people's sins. This pagan act of worship also set the stage for the final judgment and destruction of the nation as foretold in the book of Leviticus:

> Ye shall therefore keep my statutes and my judgments, and shall not commit any of these abominations; neither any of your own nation, nor any stranger that sojourneth among you: (For all these abominations have the men of the land done,

> which were before you, and the land is defiled;)
> That the land spue not you out also, when ye defile
> it, as it spued out the nations that were before you.
> (Lev. 18:27–28)

This passage prophesies that the nation of Israel could and would be "spued…out" of the land for committing the pagan abominations of the nations who preceded them and then would be dispersed into the Gentile nations where most of them remained even in Jesus's time. (There continue to be more Jews living in the nations of the world than live in Israel to this day.) They failed to see their own Messiah, but their brethren in Israel completed the cycle by once again rejecting God. Just like Adam and Eve, just like their forefathers in the wilderness, they rejected God's rulership, forfeited his relationship, and were driven from their home.

3

The Lord Enthroned in Heaven

THE PRIMARY AND most basic premise to begin with in gaining understanding of the heavenly temple is the fact that the temple is the place not only of worship but is in reality the location of the throne of God. This is shown clearly from the following verse from Revelation (more on this scripture in chapter 8):

> And the seventh angel poured out his vial into the air; and there came a great voice out of the temple of heaven, from the throne, saying, It is done. (Rev. 16:17)

Notice that the voice is identified as coming both "out of the temple" and "from the throne," positioning the throne firmly in the temple. The Greek word *apo* is translated both "out" and "from" in this verse. This word has a base meaning of movement away from a place or position toward another place or position. This clearly indicates that the throne of God is located within the temple.

> The Lord is in his holy temple, the Lord's throne is in heaven: his eyes behold, his eyelids try, the children of men. (Ps. 11:4)

If God is in his temple and on his throne, then this leaves no doubt as to where God's throne is located and also gives us insight into the dynamics of heavenly worship and the position of God enthroned in his glory. This is vitally important in recognizing the deeper meaning of the descriptions of the heavenly temple found in the New Testament. These are seen as revelatory reflections in the Old Testament tabernacle and temple patterns.

God's instructions to Moses concerning the Tabernacle and its furnishings were very clear and concise. Moses was given not only plans but what we would call today construction specifications for the building of every item. These specifications were precise as to each and every detail, including the size, shape, construction type, ornamentation, and the exact materials to be used. In Hebrews 8, Paul gives us an insight into why these descriptions are so exacting in their detail:

> Now of the things which we have spoken this is the sum: We have such an high priest, who is set on the right hand of the throne of the Majesty in the heavens; A minister of the sanctuary, and of the true tabernacle, which the Lord pitched, and not man. For every high priest is ordained to offer gifts

and sacrifices: wherefore it is of necessity that this man have somewhat also to offer. For if he were on earth, he should not be a priest, seeing that there are priests that offer gifts according to the law: Who serve unto the example and shadow of heavenly things, as Moses was admonished of God when he was about to make the tabernacle: for, See, saith he, that thou make all things according to the pattern shewed to thee in the mount. (Heb. 8:1–5)

This particular passage is bursting with crucially important concepts. First, the picture of Christ as the great, heavenly high priest is introduced. He is ministering the atonement, which he made by his own blood. Then comes the fact that the primary focus of all worship and spiritual activity is the heavenly tabernacle and not the earthly one. Remember, this passage was written to Jewish believers. The idea that their temple was in essence only a stage prop in the greater scheme of things had to come as a rude shock to them. Here Paul is showing them, and us, that the ministry of Jesus in the heavenly temple is the quintessential element in all matters relating to the relationship of God and man.

Finally, the passage gives us a glimpse into the true nature of the earthly tabernacle and temple worship. The Shekinah glory that rested above the ark of the covenant was an earthly, physical manifestation of God's holy presence. He rested over the ark in the holiest place in the earthly tabernacle just as he was enthroned above the heavenly ark.

> And the temple of God was opened in heaven, and there was seen in his temple the ark of his testament... (Rev. 11:19)

Here again is a clear-cut description of the heavenly ark within the heavenly temple. In this picture, we see that the holy of holies and the ark became a connection point between heaven and earth just as the heavens touched earth on Mount Sinai as previously seen in Exodus 24. In this case, however, the point of contact is even more significant in that it is the ark in heaven meeting the ark on earth. Revelation 15 gives us a picture of this in a manner that is eerily (but not surprisingly) similar to the descriptions of the same phenomena from the Old Testament.

> And after that I looked, and, behold, the temple of the tabernacle of the testimony in heaven was opened: And the seven angels came out of the temple, having the seven plagues, clothed in pure and white linen, and having their breasts girded with golden girdles. And one of the four beasts gave unto the seven angels seven golden vials full of the wrath of God, who liveth for ever and ever. And the temple was filled with smoke from the glory of God, and from his power; and no man was able to enter into the temple, till the seven plagues of the seven angels were fulfilled. (Rev. 15:5–8)

Now we have an understanding of precisely what took place when God's glory was manifested in Solomon's day:

> And it came to pass, when the priests were come out of the holy place, that the cloud filled the house of the Lord, So that the priests could not stand to minister because of the cloud: for the glory of the Lord had filled the house of the Lord. (1 Kings 8:11)

When God chose to reach out to mankind through the tabernacle and, later, temple worship, he supernaturally reached through the spiritual veil that separates the spiritual and physical realms. Thus, his glory was physically manifested in the holy of holies on earth just as it was in heaven.

This gives added symbolic meaning to the veil that covered the entrance to the holiest. It was a representation of that spiritual veil that separates earth from heaven. He is showing us that just as Moses and the elders climbed Mount Sinai to fellowship with him, only those who enter in within the veil will experience his true glory and presence.

4

Entering Heavenly Places

UNDER THE OLD Testament worship system, the priests administered the various sacrifices that were brought by the people. This was accomplished in the outer court of the temple. They also went inside the holy place to carry out the requirements of those phases of the worship regimen. However, once a year, the high priest entered the holy of holies to offer the blood of the atonement sacrifice on the "mercy seat" or covering of the ark of the covenant. Hebrews 9 discusses these worship procedures and introduces the idea of Christ replacing them with his own sacrifice:

> Now when these things were thus ordained, the priests went always into the first tabernacle, accomplishing the service of God. But into the second went the high priest alone once every year, not without blood, which he offered for himself, and for the errors of the people...But Christ being come an high priest of good things to come, by a greater

and more perfect tabernacle, not made with hands, that is to say, not of this building; Neither by the blood of goats and calves, but by his own blood he entered in once into the holy place, having obtained eternal redemption for us. For if the blood of bulls and of goats, and the ashes of an heifer sprinkling the unclean, sanctifieth to the purifying of the flesh: How much more shall the blood of Christ, who through the eternal Spirit offered himself without spot to God, purge your conscience from dead works to serve the living God? (Heb. 9:6–7, 11–14)

Here we see a comparison of the sacrifices made under the law by the priests and that of Jesus Christ as our Great High Priest. This passage clearly states that the tabernacle or temple that Jesus ministered in was not made by hands, i.e., heavenly in nature. It goes on to explain that the sacrifices made under Mosaic law were far inferior because the blood sacrifice of earthly animals was inferior to that made by Jesus with his own sinless blood. It finishes with the rhetorical question that if the blood of those animal sacrifices satisfied God in the matter of sanctifying unclean vessels, how much more would the blood of Jesus's perfect sacrifice sanctify and purge us? The following chapter of Hebrews continues in this vein by pointing out that the earthly sacrificial and worship system was merely a "shadow of…things to come."

For the law having a shadow of good things to come, and not the very image of the things, can never with those sacrifices which they offered year by year continually make the comers thereunto perfect. For then would they not have ceased to be offered? because that the worshippers once purged should have had no more conscience of sins. But in those sacrifices there is a remembrance again made of sins every year. For it is not possible that the blood of bulls and of goats should take away sins. Wherefore when he cometh into the world, he saith, Sacrifice and offering thou wouldest not, but a body hast thou prepared me: In burnt offerings and sacrifices for sin thou hast had no pleasure. Then said I, Lo, I come (in the volume of the book it is written of me,) to do thy will, O God. Above when he said, Sacrifice and offering and burnt offerings and offering for sin thou wouldest not, neither hadst pleasure therein; which are offered by the law; Then said he, Lo, I come to do thy will, O God. He taketh away the first, that he may establish the second. By the which will we are sanctified through the offering of the body of Jesus Christ once for all. And every priest standeth daily ministering and offering oftentimes the same sacrifices, which can never take away sins: But this man, after he had offered one sacrifice for sins for ever, sat down on the right hand of God. (Heb. 10:1–12)

Just as the earthly high priest entered once a year into the holy of holies with the blood of the atonement sacrifice, our Great High Priest, Jesus Christ, entered once and for all into the holy of holies in the heavenly temple to atone for all mankind's sins forever. (This is not to say that all mankind will be saved; only those who accept his free gift of salvation will receive the benefit of his sacrifice.) Jesus's blood served as the sin offering, the blood of sprinkling for sanctification, and the blood of atonement for all. This was truly an all-encompassing sacrifice.

> Moreover he sprinkled with blood both the tabernacle, and all the vessels of the ministry. And almost all things are by the law purged with blood; and without shedding of blood is no remission. It was therefore necessary that the patterns of things in the heavens should be purified with these; but the heavenly things themselves with better sacrifices than these. For Christ is not entered into the holy places made with hands, which are the figures of the true; but into heaven itself, now to appear in the presence of God for us… (Heb. 9:21–24)

All aspects of the sacrificial system had to be carried out to the letter of the law, the law of Moses. Every "jot and tittle" had to be fulfilled for both the law and the requirements of a holy God's need for justice and punishment of sin to be met. In John's Gospel, we read the story of Mary Magdalene's first encounter with the risen Christ:

> Jesus saith unto her, Woman, why weepest thou? whom seekest thou? She, supposing him to be the gardener, saith unto him, Sir, if thou have borne him hence, tell me where thou hast laid him, and I will take him away. Jesus saith unto her, Mary. She turned herself, and saith unto him, Rabboni; which is to say, Master. Jesus saith unto her, Touch me not; for I am not yet ascended to my Father: but go to my brethren, and say unto them, I ascend unto my Father, and your Father; and to my God, and your God. (John 20:15–17)

Jesus had not yet ascended into the heavenly temple and presented himself, and his blood, as the perfect and final sacrifice for sin. Therefore, he could not be touched by Mary. This would have ceremonially defiled him and disqualified the sacrifice! To meet the requirements of atonement, it was necessary for him to enter the temple in heaven and have his sacrificial offering received and approved by the Father as fulfilling the demands of justice.

> Being justified freely by his grace through the redemption that is in Christ Jesus: Whom God hath set forth to be a propitiation through faith in his blood, to declare his righteousness for the remission of sins that are past, through the forbearance of God. (Rom. 3:24–25)

Here we have the word *propitiation*, which means "atonement." This word in the original Greek is hilasterion, which interestingly is translated both "propitiation" and "mercy seat" and means "to appease or conciliate to oneself." In God's eyes, the place of atonement and the blood sacrifice for atonement are part and parcel of the same thing. The mercy seat in the earthly temple was the place of God's manifest presence on earth and, as seen in the previous chapter, was the contact point between the heavenly and earthly realms. Therefore, when the earthly priest offered the blood of atonement on the earthly mercy seat, he produced a temporary atonement for man that connected with that contact point. Unfortunately, that was as far as it reached. However, when Jesus offered his blood on the heavenly mercy seat, he produced a heavenly, eternal atonement that opened the way for heaven to reach into the very hearts of mankind! Now we get a far deeper understanding of the passage:

> What? know ye not that your body is the temple of the Holy Ghost which is in you… (1 Cor. 6:19)

The point of contact between the heavenly realm and the earthly—between God and man—has radically changed. No longer is the connection residing above a physical location in a physical temple; it is residing in believer himself in the person of the Holy Spirit!

5

The Heavenly Angels

IN THE PREVIOUS chapters, we have examined the earthly and the heavenly temples and the relationship or connection between them. In this chapter, we will look at the original worshippers: the angels. This will give us an insight into the worship in heaven and a view gazing forward at things to come. Psalms 103 and 104 tell us that the heavenly angels are spirit beings and that they are primarily and fundamentally ministers doing God's bidding. The Hebrew word for *angel* is *mal-ak*—messenger, which is derived from the root word *l-ak*, meaning "to send."

> Bless the Lord, ye his angels, that excel in strength, that do his commandments, hearkening unto the voice of his word. Bless ye the Lord, all ye his hosts; ye ministers of his, that do his pleasure. (Ps. 103:20–21)
>
> Who maketh his angels spirits; his ministers a flaming fire… (Ps. 104:4)

Hebrews tells us that under the new covenant, they have been additionally tasked with the responsibility of caring for us. In these verses, we are described as "heirs of salvation," and not only are the angels shown to be inferior in nature to Christ, but they are described as "ministers" to us as believers.

> But to which of the angels said he at any time, Sit on my right hand, until I make thine enemies thy footstool? Are they not all ministering spirits, sent forth to minister for them who shall be heirs of salvation? (Heb. 1:13–14)

As we put the scriptural pieces together, we begin to see the overall view of the mosaic of what the Bible says about worship in the heavenly temple. We notice that angels are an integral part of this worship.

> And another angel came and stood at the altar, having a golden censer; and there was given unto him much incense, that he should offer it with the prayers of all saints upon the golden altar which was before the throne. And the smoke of the incense, which came with the prayers of the saints, ascended up before God out of the angel's hand. (Rev. 8:3–4)

In this passage, an angel is described as offering incense with coals of fire off the altar just as the priests in the Old Testament temple would have done. The picture of an altar with burning coals of fire shows clearly that the earthly temple was an exact replica of the heavenly one, not only in form but in function as well. Isaiah's vision of God and the heavenly temple gives an even clearer insight into this principle:

> In the year that king Uzziah died I saw also the Lord sitting upon a throne, high and lifted up, and his train filled the temple. Above it stood the seraphims: each one had six wings; with twain he covered his face, and with twain he covered his feet, and with twain he did fly. And one cried unto another, and said, Holy, holy, holy, is the Lord of hosts: the whole earth is full of his glory…Then said I, Woe is me! for I am undone; because I am a man of unclean lips, and I dwell in the midst of a people of unclean lips: for mine eyes have seen the King, the Lord of hosts. Then flew one of the seraphims unto me, having a live coal in his hand, which he had taken with the tongs from off the altar: And he laid it upon my mouth, and said, Lo, this hath touched thy lips; and thine iniquity is taken away, and thy sin purged. (Isa. 6:1–3, 5–7)

Notice that the throne of God is hovering above all else in the temple and his "train" or robe filled the heavenly temple just as his Shekinah glory filled the earthly one. The angels are seen moving about and carrying out temple functions just as in Moses's day, including the use of the same types of implements; witness the "tongs" used to carry the coal of fire from the altar. The seraphim are attending angels that minister at the altar, which is apparently in front of and beneath the throne. They are seen around the throne worshipping and praising God. This is an important additional function of the angelic hosts: their role as worshippers. Before mankind was created, they were the sole source of worship to God. There are hosts of angels of all orders constantly surrounding the throne, engaged in worship and adoration.

> For ye are not come unto the mount that might be touched, and that burned with fire...But ye are come unto mount Sion, and unto the city of the living God, the heavenly Jerusalem, and to an innumerable company of angels, To the general assembly and church of the firstborn... (Heb. 12:18, 22–23)

The Hebrew word for *seraphim* is *sarap*, meaning "to burn." In fact, the same Hebrew word is used to describe the fiery serpents Moses and the children of Israel encountered in the wilderness. It is unclear if the seraphim are characterized this way because of their fiery appearance or if it stems from their function of ministering at the burning altar.

The prophet Ezekiel gives us a description of another class of angelic beings: the cherubim. Although mentioned in Daniel and Revelation, Ezekiel 1 shows us the clearest and most elaborately descriptive look at these angelic beings:

Now it came to pass in the thirtieth year, in the fourth month, in the fifth day of the month, as I was among the captives by the river of Chebar, that the heavens were opened, and I saw visions of God... And I looked, and, behold, a whirlwind came out of the north, a great cloud, and a fire infolding itself, and a brightness was about it, and out of the midst thereof as the colour of amber, out of the midst of the fire. Also out of the midst thereof came the likeness of four living creatures. And this was their appearance; they had the likeness of a man. And every one had four faces, and every one had four wings...As for the likeness of the living creatures, their appearance was like burning coals of fire, and like the appearance of lamps: it went up and down among the living creatures; and the fire was bright, and out of the fire went forth lightning. And the living creatures ran and returned as the appearance of a flash of lightning...And above the firmament that was over their heads was the likeness of a throne, as the appearance of a sapphire stone: and upon the likeness of the throne was the likeness as the appearance of a man above upon it. And I saw as the colour of amber, as the appearance of fire round about within it, from the appearance of his loins even upward, and from the appearance of his loins even downward, I saw as it were the appearance of fire, and it had brightness round about. As the appearance of the bow that is in the cloud in the day of rain, so was the appearance of the brightness round about. This was the appearance of the likeness of the glory of the Lord. And when I saw it, I fell upon my face, and I heard a voice of one that spake. (Ezek. 1:1, 4–6, 10, 13, 26–28)

The Hebrew word used in this case is *keroob*. These are the covering angels or guardians of the throne. Ezekiel 28:14 calls Lucifer "the anointed cherub that covereth," indicating that he was, before he rebelled and fell, a member of, and perhaps the leader of, this order. We also see in verse 1 that above the angelic beings, and beneath the throne of God, was a pavement like sapphire. This corresponds exactly with the depiction of the heavenly encounter of Moses and the elders of Israel in Exodus 24:9–10, as previously mentioned in the introduction. Contained in verses 26 through 28 is a stunning picture of the cherubim and the Lord revealed in his glory. Even though the cherubim are glorious and fiery in their appearance, the overwhelming glory of the Lord dominates the scene.

There can be no doubt as to these beings' identity, as chapter 9 confirms that these angelic creatures are the cherubim:

> And the glory of the God of Israel was gone up from the cherub, whereupon he was… (Ezek. 9:3)

This passage is quite obviously describing the same living creatures as in chapter 1. Chapter 10 goes on to further describe them and illuminate their duties is the heavenly temple:

> Then I looked, and, behold, in the firmament that was above the head of the cherubims there appeared over them as it were a sapphire stone, as the appearance of the likeness of a throne. And he spake unto the man clothed with linen, and said, Go in between the wheels, even under the cherub, and fill thine hand with coals of fire from between the cherubims, and scatter them over the city. Then the glory of the Lord went up from the cherub, and stood over the threshold of the house; and the house was filled with the cloud, and the court was full of the brightness of the Lord's glory. And the sound of the cherubims' wings was heard even to the outer court, as the voice of the Almighty God when he speaketh. And it came to pass, that when he had commanded the man clothed with linen, saying, Take fire from between the wheels, from between the cherubims; then he went in, and stood beside the wheels. And one cherub stretched forth his hand from between the cherubims unto the fire that was between the cherubims, and took thereof, and put it into the hands of him that was clothed with linen: who took it, and went out. (Ezek. 10:1–7)

These verses show us the actual entering in of the Shekinah glory of the Lord into the earthly temple. The context of this passage from the previous chapter is the judgments pronounced on Israel because of the earthly temple having been defiled; therefore, it is undeniably talking about the earthly temple. The Lord rises up (verse 4) from his throne on the pavement of sapphire and moves to the threshold of the earthly temple. Once again, we see the connection point between the heavenly and the earthly in this awesome narrative.

Revelation 4 shows us another view of the cherubim, along with what is arguably the most detailed description of the throne area itself:

> After this I looked, and, behold, a door was opened in heaven: and the first voice which I heard was as it were of a trumpet talking with me; which said, Come up hither, and I will shew thee things which must be hereafter. And immediately I was in the spirit: and, behold, a throne was set in heaven, and one sat on the throne. And he that sat was to look upon like a jasper and a sardine stone: and there was a rainbow round about the throne, in sight like unto an emerald. And round about the throne were four and twenty seats: and upon the seats I saw four and twenty elders sitting, clothed in white raiment; and they had on their heads crowns of gold. And out of the throne proceeded lightnings and thunderings and voices: and there were seven lamps of fire burning before the throne, which are the seven Spirits of God. And before the throne there was a sea of glass like unto crystal: and in the midst of the throne, and round about the throne, were four beasts full of eyes before and behind. And

the first beast was like a lion, and the second beast like a calf, and the third beast had a face as a man, and the fourth beast was like a flying eagle. And the four beasts had each of them six wings about him; and they were full of eyes within: and they rest not day and night, saying, Holy, holy, holy, Lord God Almighty, which was, and is, and is to come. And when those beasts give glory and honour and thanks to him that sat on the throne, who liveth for ever and ever, The four and twenty elders fall down before him that sat on the throne, and worship him that liveth for ever and ever, and cast their crowns before the throne, saying, Thou art worthy, O Lord, to receive glory and honour and power: for thou hast created all things, and for thy pleasure they are and were created. (Rev. 4:1–11)

Here we are shown the cherubim in their role as worship leaders as they "rest not day and night" while worshipping and honoring God. There is, however, an additional facet to the scene described here. There are twenty-four "elders" also taking part in this heavenly worship service. The understanding of their identity adds a new and wonderful element to this heavenly panorama. In the Aaronic priesthood, there were twenty-four courses of priests who rotated on-and-off duty in the temple. Many theologians believe these elders represent the saints of God. Revelation 5 gives further insight into this:

> And when he had taken the book, the four beasts and four and twenty elders fell down before the Lamb, having every one of them harps, and golden vials full of odours, which are the prayers of saints. And they sung a new song, saying, Thou art worthy to take the book, and to open the seals thereof: for thou wast slain, and hast redeemed us to God by thy blood out of every kindred, and tongue, and people, and nation; And hast made us unto our God kings and priests: and we shall reign on the earth. (Rev. 5:8–10)

This description of the elders makes it obvious by the song of worship they sing that they are the redeemed of the ages. No angelic being has the testimony they possess. This puts the idea of heavenly worship in a whole new light as we see the saints joining in with the angels in this heavenly worship extravaganza! It also lends a whole new meaning to 1 Corinthians 13:12:

> For now we see through a glass, darkly; but then face to face: now I know in part; but then shall I know even as also I am known. (1 Cor. 13:12)

Our participation in the heavenly worship gives us a glimpse of another pattern of worship that can be duplicated on earth, just as the temple and its functions were. This is the pattern of worship we will be examining in the following chapters.

6

Kings and Priests

THE PREVIOUS CHAPTER examines Revelation 5 and its statement that we are made "kings and priests" by Christ's sacrifice:

> Thou (Christ) art worthy to take the book, and to open the seals thereof: for thou wast slain, and hast redeemed us to God by thy blood…And hast made us unto our God kings and priests: and we shall reign on the earth. (Rev. 5:9–10)

In this chapter, we will take this discussion further and look into the nature of this priesthood. It is obvious in verse 10 that this is a different kind of priesthood than that of Aaron and his offspring as prescribed by the law of Moses. This order of priests "reign"—a function of royalty that was entirely absent from the Aaronic priests' functions. 1 Peter 2 builds on this idea by stating that we as believers will not only be carrying out "spiritual sacrifices but are a royal priesthood"—confirming the concept from Revelation 5:10 above.

> Ye also, as lively stones, are built up a spiritual house, an holy priesthood, to offer up spiritual sacrifices, acceptable to God by Jesus Christ…But ye are a chosen generation, a royal priesthood, an holy nation, a peculiar people; that ye should shew forth the praises of him who hath called you out of darkness into his marvellous light: Which in time past were not a people, but are now the people of God: which had not obtained mercy, but now have obtained mercy. (1 Pet. 2:5, 9–10)

Revelation 1:5–6 unfolds the hierarchy of this new priesthood saying that Jesus Christ is "prince of the of the kings of the earth." It also reiterates once again the statement that we are made kings and priests.

> And from Jesus Christ, who is the faithful witness, and the first begotten of the dead, and the prince of the kings of the earth. Unto him that loved us, and washed us from our sins in his own blood, And hath made us kings and priests unto God and his Father; to him be glory and dominion for ever and ever. Amen. (Rev. 1:5–6)

If he is prince of all kings and we are made kings and priests, then logically he is prince over us in that role of priest-kings. This is an extremely important distinction as we delve into the nature of this new priesthood. Hebrews 6 takes this concept even further by stating that Christ is our "high priest."

> That by two immutable things, in which it was impossible for God to lie, we might have a strong consolation, who have fled for refuge to lay hold upon the hope set before us: Which hope we have as an anchor of the soul, both sure and stedfast, and which entereth into that within the veil; Whither the forerunner is for us entered, even Jesus, made an high priest for ever after the order of Melchisedec. (Heb. 6:18–20)

Putting this verse together with Revelation 1:5, we see that Christ is the high priest and prince over an order of priest-kings in the similitude of Melchisedec, the Old Testament king of Salem (Jerusalem) who met and blessed Abraham in Genesis 14. These verses also state that Christ has entered into the holy of holies in the heavenlies as high priest. This is vitally important to us because it was through his entering that we now have the ability to enter in. Hebrews 10 tells us that this veil was in fact his own body, which, following his advent, became the physical meeting point between heaven and earth.

> Having therefore, brethren, boldness to enter into the holiest by the blood of Jesus, By a new and living

> way, which he hath consecrated for us, through the
> veil, that is to say, his flesh; And having an high priest
> over the house of God; Let us draw near with a true
> heart in full assurance of faith… (Heb. 10:19–22)

It is important to note that under the law of Moses, there was no access to the holy of holies. Only the high priest could enter there and that only once a year on the day of Yom Kippur or atonement. The Aaronic priesthood made the way into the presence of God closed to all but the select few and that only on those appointed days. The Melchisedec priesthood, on the other hand, was an open pathway for all believers to make their way into the manifest presence of the Almighty. Hebrews 7 expands on the encounter between Abraham and Melchisedec. It introduces the idea that the Melchisedec priesthood of Christ is a continual priesthood and, as chapter 6, verse 20 points out, an eternal one, whereas the Aaronic priesthood was bound to always be temporal and changing.

> For this Melchisedec, king of Salem, priest of
> the most high God, who met Abraham returning
> from the slaughter of the kings, and blessed him;
> To whom also Abraham gave a tenth part of all;
> first being by interpretation King of righteousness,
> and after that also King of Salem, which is, King
> of peace; Without father, without mother, without
> descent, having neither beginning of days, nor end
> of life; but made like unto the Son of God; abideth

a priest continually...If therefore perfection were by the Levitical priesthood, (for under it the people received the law,) what further need was there that another priest should rise after the order of Melchisedec, and not be called after the order of Aaron? (Heb. 7:1–3, 11)

Verse 11 begins a dialogue that will continue through the next two chapters: the concept that the ministry and priesthood of Christ is superior to that of the Aaronic priesthood. It states that if the priesthood prescribed by the law was sufficient, there would have been no need for Christ to establish another Melchisedec priesthood. Chapter 8 continues this theme by indicating point by point the superiority of Christ's priesthood in all his priestly functions. It then begins to illuminate the principle of ours being a "better covenant."

> Now of the things which we have spoken this is the sum: We have such an high priest, who is set on the right hand of the throne of the Majesty in the heavens; A minister of the sanctuary, and of the true tabernacle, which the Lord pitched, and not man. For every high priest is ordained to offer gifts and sacrifices: wherefore it is of necessity that this man have somewhat also to offer. For if he were on earth, he should not be a priest, seeing that there are priests that offer gifts according to the law: Who serve unto the example and shadow of heavenly

> things, as Moses was admonished of God when he was about to make the tabernacle: for, See, saith he, that thou make all things according to the pattern shewed to thee in the mount. But now hath he obtained a more excellent ministry, by how much also he is the mediator of a better covenant, which was established upon better promises...For this is the covenant that I will make with the house of Israel after those days, saith the Lord; I will put my laws into their mind, and write them in their hearts: and I will be to them a God, and they shall be to me a people... (Heb. 8:1–6, 10)

Hebrews 9 builds on this theme by listing the various paraphernalia and stages of temple worship under the law. It then reiterates that Christ is a high priest of a "greater and more perfect tabernacle," offering his own blood to cleanse and sanctify. The way into the holy of holies was not open under the law, but now the heavenly holy of holies has been entered once and for all so that all may follow him into that place of God's presence.

> Then verily the first covenant had also ordinances of divine service, and a worldly sanctuary. For there was a tabernacle made; the first, wherein was the candlestick, and the table, and the shewbread; which is called the sanctuary. And after the second veil, the tabernacle which is called the Holiest of all; Which had the golden censer, and the ark of the covenant

overlaid round about with gold, wherein was the golden pot that had manna, and Aaron's rod that budded, and the tables of the covenant; And over it the cherubims of glory shadowing the mercyseat; of which we cannot now speak particularly. Now when these things were thus ordained, the priests went always into the first tabernacle, accomplishing the service of God. But into the second went the high priest alone once every year, not without blood, which he offered for himself, and for the errors of the people: The Holy Ghost this signifying, that the way into the holiest of all was not yet made manifest, while as the first tabernacle was yet standing...But Christ being come an high priest of good things to come, by a greater and more perfect tabernacle, not made with hands, that is to say, not of this building; Neither by the blood of goats and calves, but by his own blood he entered in once into the holy place, having obtained eternal redemption for us... It was therefore necessary that the patterns of things in the heavens should be purified with these; but the heavenly things themselves with better sacrifices than these. For Christ is not entered into the holy places made with hands, which are the figures of the true; but into heaven itself, now to appear in the presence of God for us: Nor yet that he should offer himself often, as the high priest entereth into the holy place every year with blood of others; For then must he often have suffered since the foundation of the world: but now once in the end of the world hath he appeared to put away sin by the sacrifice of himself. And as it is appointed unto men once to die, but after this the judgment: So Christ was once offered to bear the sins of many; and unto them that look for him shall he appear the second time without sin unto salvation. (Heb. 9:1–8, 11–12, 23–28)

The heavenly temple has now been "purified" with the blood of Jesus, and now all believers have not only the right as priests of this new Melchisedec order to enter but the duty and obligation to "offer spiritual sacrifices," as 1 Peter 2:5 describes this new ministry.

7

Participating in the Heavenly Worship

IN THIS CHAPTER, we will examine the interaction between the angels and the saints in the heavenly worship. Up until this point, we have concentrated on the angels' role in worship around the throne; but, as we will see in the following passages, the angelic worship will be augmented by the saints as they begin to participate in an ever-increasing way. Recognizing and studying this transition will eventually lead us to study our role in the heavenly worship while we are still on the earth! In Revelation 4, we see the first glimpse of this:

> After this I looked, and, behold, a door was opened in heaven: and the first voice which I heard was as it were of a trumpet talking with me; which said, Come up hither, and I will shew thee things which must be hereafter. And immediately I was in the spirit: and,

behold, a throne was set in heaven, and one sat on the throne…And round about the throne were four and twenty seats: and upon the seats I saw four and twenty elders sitting, clothed in white raiment; and they had on their heads crowns of gold…And before the throne there was a sea of glass like unto crystal: and in the midst of the throne, and round about the throne, were four beasts full of eyes before and behind. And the first beast was like a lion, and the second beast like a calf, and the third beast had a face as a man, and the fourth beast was like a flying eagle. And the four beasts had each of them six wings about him; and they were full of eyes within: and they rest not day and night, saying, Holy, holy, holy, Lord God Almighty, which was, and is, and is to come. And when those beasts give glory and honour and thanks to him that sat on the throne, who liveth for ever and ever, The four and twenty elders fall down before him that sat on the throne, and worship him that liveth for ever and ever, and cast their crowns before the throne, saying, Thou art worthy, O Lord, to receive glory and honour and power: for thou hast created all things, and for thy pleasure they are and were created. (Rev. 4:1–2, 4, 6–11)

In verses 1 and 2, we see a symbolic picture of the rapture. Notice the command in verse 2: "Come up hither." Before this moment, there is absolutely no mention of the saints in the heavenly realm. Beginning with verse 4, however, we see a new and powerful component of the heavenly activity: the twenty-four elders. As chapter 5 shows, these elders are a symbolic and prophetic representation of the saints. Verse 6 and 7 give John's depiction of the cherubim seen by Isaiah, Ezekiel, and Daniel. Verses 8 and 9 show the angelic worship just as the Old Testament prophets recorded the same activity. In verse 10, we see for the first time the redeemed joining in the worship and adoration directed at God. This is the beginning of a transition of how the heavenly worship is depicted. Chapter 5 goes on to show the blended worship of the angels and the saints:

> And one of the elders saith unto me, Weep not: behold, the Lion of the tribe of Juda, the Root of David, hath prevailed to open the book, and to loose the seven seals thereof. And I beheld, and, lo, in the midst of the throne and of the four beasts, and in the midst of the elders, stood a Lamb as it had been slain, having seven horns and seven eyes, which are the seven Spirits of God sent forth into all the earth. And he came and took the book out of the right hand of him that sat upon the throne. And when he had taken the book, the four beasts and four and twenty elders fell down before the Lamb, having every one of them harps, and golden vials full of odours, which are the prayers of saints. (Rev. 5:6–8)

Notice verse 8: the angels and saints are worshipping together in perfect harmony. Verse eight also tells us that the prayers of the saints are stored up in golden vials or bowls, and from this point, we see this concept repeated in various ways throughout the book of Revelation. In fact, chapter 8 goes even further to show that these vials were mixed with incense and offered on the golden altar in the heavenly temple.

> And another angel came and stood at the altar, having a golden censer; and there was given unto him much incense, that he should offer it with the prayers of all saints upon the golden altar which was before the throne. And the smoke of the incense, which came with the prayers of the saints, ascended up before God out of the angel's hand. (Rev. 8:3–4)

Here we see another example of the intermingling of earthly events with the heavenly proceedings. The prayers sent up by saints on the earth have now become an integral part of the angelic ministry in the heavenly temple. Chapter 11 takes the progression another large step forward:

> And the seventh angel sounded; and there were great voices in heaven, saying, The kingdoms of this world are become the kingdoms of our Lord, and of his Christ; and he shall reign for ever and ever. And the four and twenty elders, which sat before God on their seats, fell upon their faces, and worshipped God, Saying, We give thee thanks, O Lord God Almighty, which art, and wast, and art to come; because thou hast taken to thee thy great power, and hast reigned. (Rev. 11:15–17)

Notice verse 10: the elders fall on their faces in worship and praise toward God as before, but in contrast to previous passages, there is no mention of the angelic hosts. Here for the first time, the elders are seen worshipping alone. This step in the development of heavenly worship continues a path toward an entirely new paradigm in the heavenly order. In chapter 15, this takes an even more dramatic turn:

> And I saw another sign in heaven, great and marvellous, seven angels having the seven last plagues; for in them is filled up the wrath of God. And I saw as it were a sea of glass mingled with fire: and them that had gotten the victory over the beast, and over his image, and over his mark, and over the number of his name, stand on the sea of glass, having the harps of God. And they sing the song of Moses the servant of God, and the song of the Lamb, saying, Great and marvellous are thy works, Lord God Almighty; just and true are thy ways, thou King of saints. Who shall not fear thee, O Lord, and glorify thy name? for thou only art holy: for all nations shall come and worship before thee; for thy judgments are made manifest. And after that I looked, and, behold, the temple of the tabernacle of the testimony in heaven was opened: And the seven angels came out of the temple, having the seven plagues, clothed in pure and white linen, and having their breasts girded with golden girdles. And one of the four beasts gave unto the

> seven angels seven golden vials full of the wrath of God, who liveth for ever and ever. And the temple was filled with smoke from the glory of God, and from his power; and no man was able to enter into the temple, till the seven plagues of the seven angels were fulfilled. (Rev. 15:1–8)

Verse 2 depicts the tribulation saints. They have "gotten the victory over the beast" (the Antichrist) and are now in heaven, having been martyred. One of the four beasts or cherubim give the seven last plagues to the seven angels mentioned in verse 1, who proceed to perform their ministry. There is no other mention of angelic participation in these events, especially the worship. This trend culminates in chapter 19 as we see a shift from angelic lead worship to the saints having the preeminent position.

> And after these things I heard a great voice of much people in heaven, saying, Alleluia; Salvation, and glory, and honour, and power, unto the Lord our God: For true and righteous are his judgments: for he hath judged the great whore, which did corrupt the earth with her fornication, and hath avenged the blood of his servants at her hand. And again they said, Alleluia. And her smoke rose up for ever and ever. And the four and twenty elders and the four beasts fell down and worshipped God that sat on the throne, saying, Amen; Alleluia. (Rev. 19:2–4)

Heretofore, all mention of blended worship of angels and saints has been led by the cherubim as it has since the foundation of the world. Here, however, the redeemed are mentioned first, and therefore, leading us to understand them as having the leading role. Scripture is written with the ultimate precision that only divine inspiration could bring. Thus, this transposition of the saints and angels surely cannot be merely a happenstance or coincidence. As Hebrews 1:14 states, the angels are "ministering spirits, sent forth to minister for them who shall be heirs of salvation." Here we see the culmination of God's ultimate plan: a people who are created in his image who are "heirs of God and joint heirs with Jesus Christ" and thus have moved into a position superior to the angelic hosts.

8

At the Right Hand

IN THE PREVIOUS chapter, we examined the interaction of the saints with the angelic hosts in heavenly worship. In this chapter, we will look at the actual position and nature that we, as believers in Jesus Christ, presently have spiritually and will ultimately have bodily in our final resurrected state. To fully understand these things, it is necessary to recognize Christ's current position and our position relative to him. In Ephesians 1, the apostle Paul says that Christ's present position of authority is to be seated at the right hand of the Father in his throne.

> Which he wrought in Christ, when he raised him from the dead, and set him at his own right hand in the heavenly places, Far above all principality, and power, and might, and dominion, and every name that is named, not only in this world, but also in that which is to come: And hath put all things under his feet, and gave him to be the head over all things to the church… (Eph. 1:20–22)

The custom of Jesus's day dictated that at any function, such as a feast, the guest of greatest honor would be seated at the right hand of the person hosting the event at the head table, which would normally be on a raised platform. Other honored guests would sit at the head table with the host, according to a very strictly observed protocol. Other lesser guests would be seated at other tables according to their social "rank." In Ephesians 2, Paul goes on to pen the amazing statement that we have been raised up spiritually and seated with him in his throne.

> Even when we were dead in sins, hath quickened us together with Christ, (by grace ye are saved;) And hath raised us up together, and made us sit together in heavenly places in Christ Jesus. (Eph. 2:5–6)

Notice that the tense of all the verbs in these verses are rendered in the past tense. In the original Greek, however, they are in the aorist tense. This tense focuses on the act itself without regard for past, present, or future. This example corresponds to the Greek "inceptive aorist" tense, which is primarily an indication of an event that has begun at some point in time. Therefore, we know that the action (our being enthroned with Christ) has begun, but we also know that it has not yet completed because we are not yet physically in heaven. In chapter 7, we looked at the following passage in light of our rapturing out of the earth and being taken to heaven. Now notice that in John's vision, the twenty-four elders (the saints) are depicted as already having been enthroned with Christ.

> After this I looked, and, behold, a door was opened in heaven: and the first voice which I heard was as it were of a trumpet talking with me; which said, Come up hither, and I will shew thee things which must be hereafter. And immediately I was in the spirit: and, behold, a throne was set in heaven, and one sat on the throne. And he that sat was to look upon like a jasper and a sardine stone: and there was a rainbow round about the throne, in sight like unto an emerald. And round about the throne were four and twenty seats: and upon the seats I saw four and twenty elders sitting, clothed in white raiment; and they had on their heads crowns of gold. (Rev. 4:1–4)

In this case, the Greek is in the present tense, indicating once again that when John arrived in heaven in his vision that the saints were already enthroned spiritually. From this point in time, however, they will be physically, bodily enthroned in their resurrection bodies. Verse 4 also shows us a picture of the elders presently clothed in their white raiment and with crowns on their heads, indicating that they are already enthroned as "kings and priests."

There is another aspect of our new nature as believers that needs to be addressed at this point: our position as children of God. Galatians 3 tells us that we are children of God by faith in Christ.

> For ye are all the children of God by faith in Christ Jesus. For as many of you as have been baptized into Christ have put on Christ. (Gal. 3:26–27)

Romans 8 tells us even more: we are adopted, literally "sons appointed" in the Greek, as sons and daughters of God.

> For ye have not received the spirit of bondage again to fear; but ye have received the Spirit of adoption, whereby we cry, Abba, Father. The Spirit itself beareth witness with our spirit, that we are the children of God: And if children, then heirs; heirs of God, and joint-heirs with Christ; if so be that we suffer with him, that we may be also glorified together. (Rom. 8:15–17)

Notice that we are called heirs of God and joint heirs with Christ. Hence, we as represented by the twenty-four elders, are placed in positions of great honor around the throne with God and Christ. This is the final inheritance of the saints: to be a part of the rulership of the universe with the Trinity. (Revelation 20:6 and 22:5 both show the saints reigning with him.)

The next chapter describes the process by which this exalted place is achieved. By grafting the Gentiles into the covenants, as chapter 11 terms it, God has made an entirely new and unique people for himself.

> What if God, willing to shew his wrath, and to make his power known, endured with much longsuffering the vessels of wrath fitted to destruction: And that he might make known the riches of his glory on the vessels of mercy, which he had afore prepared unto glory, Even us, whom he hath called, not of the Jews only, but also of the Gentiles? As he saith also in Osee, I will call them my people, which were not my people; and her beloved, which was not beloved. And it shall come to pass, that in the place where it was said unto them, Ye are not my people; there shall they be called the children of the living God. (Rom. 9:22–26)

We are once again called "the children of God." First John 3 takes this concept even further by shedding light on our new nature in the resurrection state.

> Behold, what manner of love the Father hath bestowed upon us, that we should be called the sons of God: therefore the world knoweth us not, because it knew him not. Beloved, now are we the sons of God, and it doth not yet appear what we shall be: but we know that, when he shall appear, we shall be like him. (1 John 3:1–2)

Now that it is becoming clearer that we have a sort of heavenly "dual citizenship," in the next chapter, we will delve into the great mystery of how we communicate between this realm and that one while we are still bound in our physical bodies. First Peter 1 tells us that even the angels "desire to look into" these mysteries!

> Unto whom it was revealed, that not unto themselves, but unto us they did minister the things, which are now reported unto you by them that have preached the gospel unto you with the Holy Ghost sent down from heaven; which things the angels desire to look into. (1 Pet. 1:12)

9

The Veil Is Torn

In chapter 8, we have seen that we have a spiritual dual citizenship in which we are spiritually residing in the heavenlies even as we are physically bound to the earth. The angels desired to "look into" these things but were prohibited from entering within the veil; only the High Priest and God himself were allowed to interact and commune there and that only once a year on the Day of Atonement. When Christ died on the cross, however, the way was opened for all to enter by his sacrificial offering of his own body and blood.

> Jesus, when he had cried again with a loud voice, yielded up the ghost. And, behold, the veil of the temple was rent in twain from the top to the bottom; and the earth did quake, and the rocks rent. (Matt. 27:50–51)

Up until this point, all worship and ministry was carried out secondhand by an earthly priesthood. We have already seen in previous chapters the superiority of the new Melchisedec priesthood. This is a heavenly priesthood with Christ enthroned in heaven as its High Priest and King of kings, and the saints enthroned with him spiritually as "kings and priests." Whereas the Aaronic priesthood carried out ministry secondhand, the Melchisedec priesthood ministers before God face-to-face.

> For we know in part, and we prophesy in part. But when that which is perfect is come, then that which is in part shall be done away. When I was a child, I spake as a child, I understood as a child, I thought as a child: but when I became a man, I put away childish things. For now we see through a glass, darkly; but then face to face: now I know in part; but then shall I know even as also I am known. (1 Cor. 13:9–12)

Why is this ministry face-to-face? Because we have already entered into the heavenly temple! If God's throne is in the heavenly temple as we saw earlier in chapter 3 and we are enthroned with him, then we are now presently ministering in that heavenly temple just as Jesus is! Notice that Hebrews 6:20 calls him our "forerunner."

> Wherein God, willing more abundantly to shew unto the heirs of promise the immutability of his counsel, confirmed it by an oath: That by two immutable things, in which it was impossible for God to lie, we might have a strong consolation, who

have fled for refuge to lay hold upon the hope set before us: Which hope we have as an anchor of the soul, both sure and stedfast, and which entereth into that within the veil; Whither the forerunner is for us entered, even Jesus, made an high priest for ever after the order of Melchisedec. (Heb. 6:17–20)

Romans 8:29 calls him the "firstborn among many brethren." Colossians 1:18 says "he is the head of the body, the church: who is the beginning, the firstborn from the dead; that in all things he might have the preeminence." The veil was torn to open the way for the new priesthood to enter in and begin their priestly duties. The old priesthood only went into the holy place; the holy of holies was off limits to all but the high priest. Under the new priesthood, the holy of holies was opened to all. Hebrews 9 tells us that the old system of worship, as embodied in the "first tabernacle," was a "figure for the time then present." It goes on to describe his priesthood ministry role within the veil:

> Now when these things were thus ordained, the priests went always into the first tabernacle, accomplishing the service of God. But into the second went the high priest alone once every year, not without blood, which he offered for himself, and for the errors of the people: The Holy Ghost this signifying, that the way into the holiest of all was not yet made manifest, while as the first tabernacle was yet standing: Which was a figure for the time

> then present, in which were offered both gifts and sacrifices, that could not make him that did the service perfect, as pertaining to the conscience; Which stood only in meats and drinks, and divers washings, and carnal ordinances, imposed on them until the time of reformation. But Christ being come an high priest of good things to come, by a greater and more perfect tabernacle, not made with hands, that is to say, not of this building; Neither by the blood of goats and calves, but by his own blood he entered in once into the holy place, having obtained eternal redemption for us. For if the blood of bulls and of goats, and the ashes of an heifer sprinkling the unclean, sanctifieth to the purifying of the flesh: How much more shall the blood of Christ, who through the eternal Spirit offered himself without spot to God, purge your conscience from dead works to serve the living God? (Heb. 9:6–14)

Hebrews 10 tells us that Christ not only entered through the veil but that the physical veil was in fact his own flesh. The spiritual veil into the holy of holies was breached by the tearing of his own flesh in his sacrificial death.

> This is the covenant that I will make with them after those days, saith the Lord, I will put my laws into their hearts, and in their minds will I write them; And their sins and iniquities will I remember no more. Now where remission of these is, there is no more offering for sin. Having therefore, brethren,

boldness to enter into the holiest by the blood of Jesus, By a new and living way, which he hath consecrated for us, through the veil, that is to say, his flesh; And having an high priest over the house of God; Let us draw near with a true heart in full assurance of faith… (Heb. 10:16–22)

Just as Christ now ministers as King and High Priest within the veil, we now also minister within the veil as priest-kings of the new order. Revelation 1 calls him the "Prince of the kings of the earth." The Greek word used here is *archon*, which means "chief ruler." He is the ruler and head of all powers and authorities. The passage goes on to reiterate that we have been "made" kings and priests. The word *made* indicates an appointing and supervising authority.

> And from Jesus Christ, who is the faithful witness, and the first begotten of the dead, and the prince of the kings of the earth. Unto him that loved us, and washed us from our sins in his own blood, And from Jesus Christ, who is the faithful witness, and the first begotten of the dead, and the prince of the kings of the earth. Unto him that loved us, and washed us from our sins in his own blood, And hath made us kings and priests unto God and his Father; to him be glory and dominion for ever and ever. Amen. Behold, he cometh with clouds; and every eye shall see him, and they also which pierced him: and all kindreds of the earth shall wail because of him. Even so, Amen. (Rev. 1:5–7)

Having seen the fullness of the ministry derived from our appointment as kings and priests, we begin to get a fuller picture of heavenly worship. To summarize,

God is enthroned in the heavenly temple above the heavenly ark.

Christ is enthroned at God's right hand, ministering as the Great High Priest of the new Melchisedec priesthood.

We are enthroned with Christ, seated in heavenly places, ministering in our role as kings and priests of this new priesthood.

Just as Moses and Aaron entered the heavenlies and trod on the pavement of sapphire to commune with God, we have the perpetual right to come before the Father and commune with him, offering our sacrifices of worship and praise and presenting our petitions.

Our ministry in the heavenly temple is face-to-face and hindered only by the veil of our flesh, which restrains us from the fullness of worship and fellowship we will have when Christ returns and we receive our glorified immortal bodies. Then we will be resident in the heavenlies, not only spiritually but physically as well.

10

Davidic Worship

Second Samuel 6 portrays one of the seminal events of King David's reign: the bringing of the ark of the covenant into Jerusalem. The tabernacle was stationed at Gibeon, about ten miles from Jerusalem as the crow flies.

> For the tabernacle of the Lord, which Moses made in the wilderness, and the altar of the burnt offering, were at that season in the high place at Gibeon. But David could not go before it to enquire of God: for he was afraid because of the sword of the angel of the Lord. (1 Chron. 21:29–30)

David had attempted to bring it to Jerusalem once previously, but the incident involving Uzzah's death (2 Sam. 6) for touching the ark had frightened him away from the idea. He then learned that Obededom's household, where the ark was left after the death of Uzzah, was being abundantly blessed because of the ark's presence.

> And it was told king David, saying, The Lord hath blessed the house of Obededom, and all that pertaineth unto him, because of the ark of God. So David went and brought up the ark of God from the house of Obededom into the city of David with gladness. And it was so, that when they that bare the ark of the Lord had gone six paces, he sacrificed oxen and fatlings. And David danced before the Lord with all his might; and David was girded with a linen ephod. So David and all the house of Israel brought up the ark of the Lord with shouting, and with the sound of the trumpet. (2 Sam. 6:12–15)

David was not naked, as some interpreters contend, but wore a linen ephod (a priestly garment). This linen ephod is a clear identification of his function during the bringing in of the ark as priestly in nature. In 1 Samuel 22, when King Saul orders the execution of a group of priests, they are specifically referenced as wearing a linen ephod.

> And the king said to Doeg, Turn thou, and fall upon the priests. And Doeg the Edomite turned, and he fell upon the priests, and slew on that day fourscore and five persons that did wear a linen ephod… (1 Sam. 22:19)

This would have been the same type of ephod or priestly tunic worn by Samuel as a boy priest:

> But Samuel ministered before the Lord, being a child, girded with a linen ephod. Moreover his mother made him a little coat, and brought it to him from year to year, when she came up with her husband to offer the yearly sacrifice. (1 Sam. 2:18–20)

When David wore this ephod, he had lain aside his royal raiment for that of a priest. This was the same garment worn by all priests to perform their priestly duties. By bringing the ark into Jerusalem in this manner, David was reinstituting the Melchisedec priesthood of the priest-king!

> And David made him houses in the city of David, and prepared a place for the ark of God, and pitched for it a tent...And David gathered all Israel together to Jerusalem, to bring up the ark of the Lord unto his place, which he had prepared for it...And David was clothed with a robe of fine linen, and all the Levites that bare the ark, and the singers, and Chenaniah the master of the song with the singers: David also had upon him an ephod of linen. Thus all Israel brought up the ark of the covenant of the Lord...So they brought the ark of God, and set it in the midst of the tent that David had pitched for it: and they offered burnt sacrifices and peace offerings before God. (1 Chron. 15:1, 3;27–28, 16:1)

This verse tells us that David not only had on an ephod but was wearing underneath it a "robe of fine linen." The

Hebrew word here is *meh-eel*. This word has among its usages that of the robe worn by the High Priest. Now we see an even stronger indication of his intention to step into the role of priest-king.

As chapter 2 points out, the nation of Israel rebelled against God at Mount Sinai and rejected him. This ended the personal face-to-face type of relationship that Moses and Abraham had with the Lord and initiated a secondhand relationship and, thereby, a secondhand worship via the Aaronic priesthood. Now, in this scenario, David is reinstituting the original form of interaction with God with what scripture calls the tabernacle of David. The ark rested under a simple tent and was open to all. Without realizing it, David was creating a prophetic forerunner of the New Testament model of worship and ministry. When he entered Jerusalem in the king-priest role, he set in motion a chain of events that could have potentially restored the pre-Mosaic pattern of worship. But it was not to be. As the following passage shows, David desired to build a "house" for God, and once again, human effort replaced divine relationship.

> And it came to pass, when the king sat in his house, and the Lord had given him rest round about from all his enemies; That the king said unto Nathan the prophet, See now, I dwell in an house of cedar, but the ark of God dwelleth within curtains. And Nathan said to the king, Go, do all that is in thine heart; for the Lord is with thee. And it came to pass that

night, that the word of the Lord came unto Nathan, saying, Go and tell my servant David, Thus saith the Lord, Shalt thou build me an house for me to dwell in? Whereas I have not dwelt in any house since the time that I brought up the children of Israel out of Egypt, even to this day, but have walked in a tent and in a tabernacle. In all the places wherein I have walked with all the children of Israel spake I a word with any of the tribes of Israel, whom I commanded to feed my people Israel, saying, Why build ye not me an house of cedar?…And as since the time that I commanded judges to be over my people Israel, and have caused thee to rest from all thine enemies. Also the Lord telleth thee that he will make thee an house. And when thy days be fulfilled, and thou shalt sleep with thy fathers, I will set up thy seed after thee, which shall proceed out of thy bowels, and I will establish his kingdom. He shall build an house for my name, and I will stablish the throne of his kingdom for ever. I will be his father, and he shall be my son… (2 Sam. 7:1–5, 6–7, 11–14)

God gave David, and later Solomon, permission to build a temple; but these verses are clear that the construction of a temple was not God's priority. Notice that after the Lord rhetorically asks, "Shalt thou build me an house for me to dwell in?" he goes on to ask David when he ever asked the nation to build him a house. God then proceeds to say in verse 11 that he would make David a house. God's focus was on the lineage of Messiah and the priesthood he would establish, not the physical structure David wanted to erect.

The temple was built, and this style of worship encounter with God was lost. Amos, however, foretold a day that will see the restoration of the tabernacle of David and Davidic worship.

> In that day will I raise up the tabernacle of David that is fallen, and close up the breaches thereof; and I will raise up his ruins, and I will build it as in the days of old...And I will bring again the captivity of my people of Israel, and they shall build the waste cities, and inhabit them; and they shall plant vineyards, and drink the wine thereof; they shall also make gardens, and eat the fruit of them. And I will plant them upon their land, and they shall no more be pulled up out of their land which I have given them, saith the Lord thy God. (Amos 9:11, 14–15)

The wording of this passage clearly dates it as an end-time scenario. The theme of the restoration of Israel in their land labels this as an end-time/millennial prophecy. We can see from these verses that the worship style in the millennial kingdom would be Davidic in nature. Jeremiah also prophesied of this period that there will be no more mention of the ark of the covenant, i.e., Aaronic/Mosaic worship. The throne of the Lord in his kingdom will be the focal point of all nations.

> And it shall come to pass, when ye be multiplied and increased in the land, in those days, saith the Lord, they shall say no more, The ark of the covenant of the Lord: neither shall it come to mind: neither shall they remember it; neither shall they visit it; neither shall that be done any more. At that time they shall call Jerusalem the throne of the Lord; and all the nations shall be gathered unto it, to the name of the Lord, to Jerusalem: neither shall they walk any more after the imagination of their evil heart. In those days the house of Judah shall walk with the house of Israel, and they shall come together out of the land of the north to the land that I have given for an inheritance unto your fathers. (Jer. 3:16–18)

Isaiah prophesied of the coming of Messiah to take up the throne of David. Notice, however, that the throne it refers to will be in the tabernacle of David! In the millennial kingdom, the ark, which was the place of God's manifest presence, will be replaced with Christ's personal presence.

> And in mercy shall the throne be established: and he shall sit upon it in truth in the tabernacle of David, judging, and seeking judgment, and hasting righteousness. (Isa. 16:5)

This leaves us with the obvious question: in light of this, how should we, as believers, worship now?

11

Bringing in the Glory

IN THE PREVIOUS chapter, we saw David laid aside his kingly garments for the garb of not only a priest but the High Priest. In Mark's account of Jesus's triumphal entry into Jerusalem, we see a similar phenomenon.

> And they brought the colt to Jesus, and cast their garments on him; and he sat upon him. And many spread their garments in the way: and others cut down branches off the trees, and strawed them in the way. And they that went before, and they that followed, cried, saying, Hosanna; Blessed is he that cometh in the name of the Lord: Blessed be the kingdom of our father David, that cometh in the name of the Lord: Hosanna in the highest. And Jesus entered into Jerusalem, and into the temple: and when he had looked round about upon all things, and now the eventide was come, he went out unto Bethany with the twelve. (Mark 11:7–11)

The disciples and followers remove their robes and spread them over the pathway. This prophetic act recalls that of David. Just as he symbolically stripped himself of his righteousness and glory to bring in the ark, the symbol of God's presence, they removed their outward covering and laid them at his feet in an act of humility before his presence.

Jesus immediately went into the temple, indicating that the priority at that time was his priestly function rather than the kingly. His kingly office will not be fulfilled until he returns to set up his millennial kingdom. In the meantime, he is seated at the right hand of his Father, waiting until the fullness of time to return and take up the throne of David.

> And in mercy shall the throne be established: and he shall sit upon it in truth in the tabernacle of David, judging, and seeking judgment, and hasting righteousness. (Isa. 16:5)

Notice that the throne of Christ in the millennial reign is in the tabernacle of David. The ark, as chapter 10 points out, will no longer be visited or even remembered. Jesus himself will be enthroned in that tabernacle as both King and High Priest. The mercy seat that covered the ark will no longer be needed as he is both the sacrifice of atonement and the covering for all. In fact, the identical Greek word is used for atonement and for mercy seat.

Here we see a pattern emerge. Jesus is enthroned temporarily in heaven, waiting to be enthroned in the tabernacle of David in lieu of a temple. We have seen in previous chapters that God is enthroned in the heavenly temple. Psalm 11 makes this abundantly clear.

> The Lord is in his holy temple, the Lord's throne is in heaven: his eyes behold, his eyelids try, the children of men. (Ps. 11:4)

Where then is the throne of the Holy Spirit to complete the enthronement of the Trinity? An examination of scripture will show that the Holy Spirit's throne is in the heart of the believer.

> Know ye not that ye are the temple of God, and that the Spirit of God dwelleth in you? (1 Cor. 3:16)

And again,

> For we know that if our earthly house of this tabernacle were dissolved, we have a building of God, an house not made with hands, eternal in the heavens.

These passages not only call us both temples and tabernacles but indicate that the dwelling place of the Holy Spirit on earth is in our hearts. If we are temples and at the same time we are priest-kings of the renewed Melchisedec priesthood, then we need to realize that we are walking, talking worship events every day in every place we go and in everything we do. This is the crux of Davidic worship. The worship is within us in direct and open communication with God through the Holy Spirit as our intercessor and by way of Jesus as our mediator. Just as the tabernacle of David was open to all, the way within the veil has been opened and all the redeemed may enter freely.

> What? know ye not that your body is the temple of the Holy Ghost which is in you, which ye have of God, and ye are not your own? For ye are bought with a price: therefore glorify God in your body, and in your spirit, which are God's. (1 Cor. 6:19–20)

Notice the phrase "therefore glorify God." Based on these facts, all our existence should focused on our priesthood of worship, praise, and sharing the good news of the kingdom with all those within our circle of influence.

> Ye also, as lively stones, are built up a spiritual house, an holy priesthood, to offer up spiritual sacrifices, acceptable to God by Jesus Christ. (1 Pet. 2:5)

What are these "spiritual sacrifices"? Hosea 14:2 says we should "render the calves of our lips," indicating that there will be no need for physical, animal sacrifices anymore. All future sacrifices under the new covenant will be those that come from within our hearts, i.e., the throne of the Holy Spirit within us. Just as the ark was the connection point to the heavenly temple in the old covenant, our indwelt spirit, our ark in our "temple," is the connection point to the Trinity under the new covenant. This is the true nature of worship in the heavenly temple. We are priest-kings carrying out our appointed tasks as worshippers, intercessors, and praise leaders co-laboring with the angelic hosts in the ministry before God on his throne. All this ministry is inspired by the Holy Spirit within us. Jesus receives the honor and praise rising up and funnels it on to the Father. He in turn pours out his power and anointing on us to accomplish even greater ministry, completing the circuit of divine delegation of power and authority.

> As every man hath received the gift, even so minister the same one to another, as good stewards of the manifold grace of God. If any man speak, let him speak as the oracles of God; if any man minister, let him do it as of the ability which God giveth: that God in all things may be glorified through Jesus Christ, to whom be praise and dominion for ever and ever. Amen. (1 Pet. 4:11)

All our attention should be focused on ministering to him and all our ability directed toward ministering to others. This is the heart of the priesthood of the heavenly temple.

> *For of him, and through him, and to him, are all things: to whom be glory for ever. Amen. (Rom. 11:36)*

www.ingramcontent.com/pod-product-compliance
Lightning Source LLC
Chambersburg PA
CBHW070544300426
44113CB00011B/1782